Victor Adeyemi

ENTER YOUR REST!

Pathway to Supernatural Success

Unless otherwise indicated, all scripture quotations are taken from the *King James Version* of the Bible.

Enter Your Rest

ISBN 978-978-52323-0-1

First Print 2013
Second Print 2018

A publication Harvest House.
G.P.O. BOX 37693 Ibadan,
Oyo State Nigeria.
+234 818 888 8826
info@victoradeyemi.org
www.victoradeyemi.org

To

Global Harvest Church members worldwide

Acknowledgements

MY GRATITUDE GOES to Pastor Bryce Edem for editing the original manuscripts. '*Thank you for your toil over this book*'.

My unquantifiable gratitude to the staff of Victor Adeyemi Ministries led by Nathaniel Adegoke for your timeless efforts to see this book through transcription, editing and printing. '*May your labor of love be abundantly rewarded*'.

I also want to appreciate the love of my life, *Jumoke*, whose constant love, encouragement and support keeps me productive in God's vineyard.

Table of Contents

Introduction

There is a paradigm shift from the Old Testament to the New. The Old Testament starts with a big 'do' while the New Testaments starts with a big 'done'! The liberty that the New Testament of grace affords needs to be understood and appropriated.

I am often amazed at the degree of toil that characterizes the average Christian life these days from our frantic efforts to live holy lives, to our struggles to succeed in our vocations; the advantage of the Christian life over the unchristian one is hardly noticeable!

My burden in presenting this book is an attempt to present a manual to the seeking heart, hopefully to find a place of security in God, where the daily life of faith becomes a practical, delightful and successful experience.

This certainly was God's original intention as He ushered man into a world of bliss devoid of toil and struggle. He created man on the sixth day and made the seventh day (man's first day), a day of rest. Rest is still on God's mind for every of His children.

> *Man rested in God's work before he began to work for God!*

Working for God while resting in Him is the way to go and I hope that the following pages will show you how.

Welcome to your rest…

Victor Adeyemi

Chapter 1

Invitation To Rest

Hebrews 3: 7-11…

> ***'Wherefore (as the Holy Ghost saith, today if ye will hear his voice, Harden not your hearts, as in the provocation, in the day of temptation in the wilderness: When your fathers tempted me, proved me, and saw my works forty years. Wherefore I was grieved with that generation, and said, they do alway err in their heart; and they have not known my ways. So I sware in my wrath, they shall not enter into my rest)'.***

Hebrews 4:3-4

> ***'For we which have believed do enter into rest, as he said, as I have sworn in my wrath, if they***

> ***shall enter into my rest: although the works were finished from the foundation of the world. For he spake in a certain place of the seventh day on this wise, And God did rest the seventh day from all his works'.***

I would like you to note that the promise of rest is not an automatic promise. That a promise is made does not necessarily guaranty everyone would receive what is promised. According to the scriptures, God had made a promise that He would give the land of Canaan to Israel. Sadly, many of them did not appropriate that promise to themselves.

Our second cardinal scripture passage in this chapter seems to be quite unsettling and perhaps, confusing. When work is finished, rest naturally follows. But not in the case cited in the scripture I am referring to here. The word of God says that God had finished His work, yet some people did not enter into rest. Rest is cessation from work or labour. But how could work had finished and the people still did not rest?

Here's the simple reason: it is possible not to rest on the finished work! My personal discovery is that rest which comes from God is predicated on embracing God's finished work. In other words, it has been done already. What has been done, has been done. Once it was performed, it was performed. Once it had been implemented, it had been implemented. It is a done deal.

There are three dimensions to this finished work:

1. The Finished Work of Eternity

Whenever we hear the word 'eternity' our minds always race forward. To create a construct of eternity in the future sense is absolutely correct. But to create a construct of eternity only in the future sense is abysmally incorrect. There is more to eternity that just the future. There is eternity ahead no doubt but there is also eternity past. Eternity speaks of timelessness. Before time began, there was a period of timelessness–a period when time did not exist or count.

The Bible in *Genesis 1: 1* say

> ***'In the beginning God created the heaven and the ea rth'.***

John 1:1 says

> ***'In the beginning was the Word, and the Word was with God, and the Word was God'.***

Both verses speak about a particular period of timelessness. If the Hebrew language had correctly translated those passages, we would realize that God did not create the heaven and earth in the beginning. He created the heaven and earth in the timeless past. The beginning of the measurement of time is found in *Genesis 1:3-5*, which says;

> ***'And God said, Let there be light: and there was light. And God saw the light, that it was good: and God divided the light from the darkness. And***

> ***God called the light Day, and the darkness he called Night. And the evening and the morning were the first day'.***

That was the beginning of the count of time. But before this beginning, there was timelessness. The Bible tells us that, in that season of timelessness, God did a particular work. According to *Revelation 13:8*

> ***'And all that dwell upon the earth shall worship him, whose names are not written in the book of life of the Lamb slain from the foundation of the world'.***

Jesus is the one being described as the lamb and the verse also talks about those who were rejected by God, whose names were not written in The Book of Life of The Lamb slain from the foundation of the world. Jesus Christ was slain in eternity past. He was slain in the plan and the programme of God. God had planned and programmed everything in the realm of the spirit. He finished everything about it before He started to implement it. Even before Jesus was born, was a done deal!

John the Baptist also made the same statement when Jesus came to him to be baptized. In *Luke Chapter 3*, John said *'Behold the lamb of God slain from the foundation of the world'.*

John said Jesus was already slain before he was actually slain. Jesus was physically slain at Calvary more than 2000 years ago but He had been slain long before the foundation of the world. You are here today according to a programme that was

set before the foundation of the world. God has books. God's books and records were written before the foundation of the world. The Psalmist says…

> ***'My substance was not hid from thee, when I was made in secret, and curiously wrought in the lowest parts of the earth. Thine eyes did see my substance, yet being unperfect; and in thy book all my members were written, which in continuance were fashioned, when as yet there was none of them'…***
>
> *Psalms 139:15-16.*

Here, David spoke figuratively about his conception and development in his mother's womb. How did the Psalmist say God saw his formation? It was according to what was written in God's book. Your life was written before it was formed.

According to *Jeremiah 1:5*

> ***'Before I formed thee in the belly I knew thee; and before thou camest forth out of the womb I sanctified thee, and I ordained thee a prophet unto the nations'.***

This implies that God already knew you before your formation. Your formation was according to what was written. Your life was written before the foundation of the world. The question then is what was written? The Bible answers this question in *Jeremiah 29:11…*

> ***'For I know the thoughts that I think toward you, saith the LORD, thoughts of peace, and not of evil, to give you an expected end'.***

This is the plan God has for you. It is a plan to give you peace and not evil. It is a plan for prosperity, not a plan of scarcity. It is a plan to make you successful, not to make you a failure. That was written concerning you before the foundation of the world. You must embrace this truth and rest on that reality. This is a bold, audacious, royal invitation to rest on God's finished work.

You never would have come into this world if you hadn't been passed as successful. You never would have been conceived in the first instance if in God's grand design and detailed programme, you had not been completed in eternity and certified victorious. You must rest on this knowledge.

Jeremiah 1:5 says

> ***'Before you were formed in the belly I knew you, before you came out of your mother's belly I sanctified and ordained you a prophet unto the nations'.***

Jeremiah was ordained to be a prophet before was conceived in his mother's womb! It was a carefully sketched and properly designed plan from the foundation of the world. So, I want you to know that you are not here, buying time or occupying space. Neither are you just a number in the crowd. You do not just make up the statistics. You are a distinct person with a unique

plan of God for your life. That plan was already completed, everything about it–who you would be, where you would be, to the minutest details.

All the provisions that you will need to succeed at what you were designed and fashioned for have already been released. You will win, succeed and prosper because of what has already been written in the timeless past. Those who rest on what has been written enjoy what has been written; those who do not rest on it, do not enjoy it.

Until your attitude changes to align with this truth, rest would be far from you. Until your attitude becomes that of total reliance on God, trusting that His mighty hand is upon your life, you will not enjoy rest. Do not let your present situation and circumstance dictate to you. If things are working well, it is according to plan. If nothing seems to work, it is a lie! Even The Lamb that was slain from the foundation of the world faced challenges when He came into the world. Was everything rosy for Jesus Christ? No! He ran away from cities because people planned to kill Him. He was lied against, falsely accused, indicted, crucified–but all was according to plan. So, rest in the finished work of eternity past.

2. Rest in the Finished Work of Creation

> ***'For he spake in a certain place of the seventh day on this wise, And God did rest the seventh day from all his works'...***
>
> *Hebrews 4: 4.*

The idea in scripture is that once God began to rest on the seventh day, He has remained in that state of rest till now. You wonder why? This is because the works were all finished. They were all finished in potential form: the cars had been created, the airplanes had been created and everything else you can think of!

The raw materials for their creation were all in the land that God separated from the waters in *Genesis 1*. The clothes were inside the trees. At creation, everything was in potential form, awaiting physical manifestation. So everything you will ever need–financially, physically and materially–was already made.

Your body was in the soil. Your spirit was inside Adam. When Adam was created, all humans were created too. The work was already completed from the beginning. The fact that God rested means that work was done and the work was finished. Everything was already successful. Failure was impossible. The job was accomplished! Halleulyah!

The Bible says

> ***'For we which have believed do enter into rest, as he said, As I have sworn in my wrath, if they shall enter into my rest: although the works were finished from the foundation of the world'....***
>
> *Hebrew 4:3.*

God did not ask you to enter your own rest but to enter His own rest. How can you enter into somebody else's rest? You can only enter into someone else's rest if that person had already

worked for you and you are just invited to come and share in the success. It means that someone did the work and is inviting you to come and share in the reward. Isn't this wonderful?

When at creation God worked from the first to the sixth day, He did not only work for that moment. He worked for the future and worked till the end of time. Human beings born into this world are to enter into that finished work. Entering into that rest is first and foremost an attitude–attitude of tranquility, relaxation, peace and total trust in what had been done.

Christianity does not begin with a big 'Do', it begins with a big 'Done'. Do you know that it was after Adam had sinned that God told him that henceforth he would toil to eat and would only eat from the sweat of his brow? How did Adam eat before this repercussion of sin was pronounced? The answer is pretty simple: He was eating without toil.

Does this mean he was lazy? No. He was working but he was working without toiling because he entered into the finished work. Everything he did inside the Garden of Eden was by grace. It was not him struggling but God at work through him. Adam was created on the sixth day and on the seventh day God rested. So Adam's life began with rest, implying that God made him to rest first before he did any work.

This invitation to rest is to partner with God with an attitude that says 'success is already guaranteed'. It is when you do not believe that rest is guaranteed that you would be anxious as to whether you would succeed or not.

3. Rest in the Finished Work of Calvary

This invitation to rest is an invitation to rest in the finished work of Calvary. ***'When Jesus therefore had received the vinegar, he said, It is finished: and he bowed his head, and gave up the ghost'***... *John 19:30*.

Which work was Jesus referring to? The work of the redemption of man from sin and all consequences of sin. *Romans 3: 23* says ***'For all have sinned, and come short of the glory of God'***.

The divine dimension in which man was operating was taken away from him when he fell short of the glory of God. Man ate from his toil as a consequence of disobedience. He had to use his own efforts, power and wisdom to get the job done once he lost the manifest presence of God in Eden. Moses told God if His presence would not go with him, he would not move a step (Exodus 33:15). He knew God's presence would make all the difference.

Jesus in *Mark 16: 17* said

> ***'And these signs shall follow them that believe; In my name shall they cast out devils; they shall speak with new tongues'***.

The word *'follow'* gives the impression that the signs will come after you but in the original Greek, it means *'to accompany'*. This implies that you should operate in signs and wonders. You should not do business without the touch of wonder on it. You should not be on your job without experiencing the touch of the supernatural. This is because the touch of man would only produce ordinary results mere mortals can achieve. But when God's touch comes on your work, it would cease to be ordinary.

When God's hand came upon Jacob's husbandry business, it transferred the wealth of Laban to him by just one divine inspiration for God's wisdom. That was the first record of genetic engineering in history. A person with Sickle Cell Anaemia can experience genotype change supernaturally. Even physical parts of the human body can be changed supernaturally. God is the creator and He can do all things. Halleluyah!

Let us learn to rest in the finished work of Calvary. Jesus went to the cross and bore the sin that caused man to come short of the glory of God. On the cross, He was separated from God and He screamed out of desperation, '*My God, my God; why hast thou forsaken me*'.

Jesus always referred to God as '*My Father*' but on the cross He assumed an intercessory role for humanity, bellowing, '*My God*'! For the first time ever, Jesus experienced what it meant to live without the presence of God! For people who have never experienced the presence of God, it might make no difference at all. You do not know what you are missing when you are not missing it. You simply cannot understand the difference!

Jesus never knew what it was like to be without His father. The presence of God was His normal, daily experience. He lived perpetually in the presence of His father and He was always anointed. The Spirit of the Lord was always upon Him. When He was born into this world, He was born into communion with The Father because He was filled with the Holy Ghost right from His mother's womb. But on the cross of Calvary He was alone and He knew what it was to be without the presence of The Father.

He was banished from the presence of God so that we might be welcomed there. He was made sin so that we might be made righteous in Christ Jesus. He was made sick so that we might be healed. He was made poor so that we might be rich. The work was finished. Every barrier between God and man is broken in Christ Jesus. The curse is broken. He has redeemed us from the curse of the law according to the Bible. *Galatians 3:13*

> ***'Christ hath redeemed us from the curse of the law, being made a curse for us: for it is written, Cursed is every one that hangeth on a tree'.***

It was written in *Deuteronomy 21:23*

> ***His body shall not remain all night upon the tree, but thou shalt in any wise bury him that day; (for he that is hanged is accursed of God;) that thy land be not defiled, which the LORD thy God giveth thee for an inheritance.***

Now, the blessing of Abraham is ours. Rest in that finished work. The Bible says ***'For the promise, that he should be the heir of the world, was not to Abraham, or to his seed, through***

the law, but through the righteousness of faith'...*Romans 4:13.*

What does *'heir of the world'* mean? It means 'the owner'. The Bible says that the promise that he will be the heir of the world was not made to Abraham and to his seed according to the law but to his seed according to the righteousness of faith. Who are the seed according to the righteousness of faith? You and I. it is referring to everyone who is born again. Hallelujah!

What is the promise that God made to Abraham and to us who are the seed through the righteousness of faith? The promise is that we own everything. Rest on that reality! If truly you are the heir of the world together with father Abraham, then all you need to fulfill your vision is settled. If for any reason it has not yet happened, it means it is not yet time for it. It is time for it but nothing can stop it from happening.

Maybe in God's programme, the appropriate times and seasons are not exact yet. Or maybe it is the issue of you not resting to receive and enjoy it. Even when you rest in the finished work, you still need patience and persistence. All things are yours. It is just a matter of time and all of them would manifest in your life. Hold on to God's unchanging Word .

Chapter 2

Labour To Enter His Rest

'It still remains that some will enter that rest, and those who formerly had the gospel preached to them did not go in, because of their disobedience'...

Hebrews 4:6.

'There remaineth therefore a rest to the people of God. For he that is entered into his rest, he also hath ceased from his own works, as God did from his. Let us labour therefore to enter into that rest, lest any man fall after the same example of unbelief'...

Hebrews 4: 9–11.

I would like to address a burning issue which I cannot gloss over as though it does not matter. I believe God is stirring my heart to write to His people on this subject. Sadly, many of God's people have swallowed 'another gospel' to their own detriment, hook, line and sinker. This has negatively affected their walk with Christ and has caused many to live below God's expectations.

Some Christians think that if they will be blessed, it must be because of their own effort. They believe that for anything to be theirs, they must work it out by themselves. They believe that only in exertion of brute strength and back-breaking toil would they have results.

This is a fallacious postulation. It is so untrue; a lie that the enemy has sold to so many Christians. Please do not misunderstand me. I believe in honest labour and hard work. I believe we should work out our dreams. Industry and diligence is a cardinal teaching in the Bible. I need to state that in clear, unmistakable terms. But if we believe that all we could ever be and have would depend exclusively on our strength and exertion of brute energy, then that assumption falls flat in the face of undeniable proofs.

The scripture passages quoted above have a few of these undeniable proofs.

The Bible clearly teaches that God longs for His people to come into His rest. The subject of rest is a recurring theme in the scriptures. The rest God gives sets aside our excessive labour and anxiety on our part. God seized from His own work. He withdrew from His labour of six days and rested on the seventh day. People who enter into God's rest seize from their labours.

The second scripture above tells us to labour to enter into that rest. At first glance and casual skimming, someone would think that statement is contradictory. But when you observe closely, you would find the contrary. What kind of labour are we commanded to expend in order to enter into God's rest?

> ***'So I sware in my wrath, they shall not enter into my rest. Take heed, brethren, lest there be in any of you an evil heart of unbelief, in departing from the living God'...***
>
> *Hebrews 3: 11–12.*

The reason why the Israelites could not enter into the rest God promised them was because of unbelief. Unbelief is a serious sin before God.

It is amazing the way people categorize sin. Most men rank murder at the highest level, followed by fornication, then theft and so on. The way even tongue-speaking, born-again Christians tell lies these days have pushed lying down the list of sin! Lying would probably rank number twenty or further lower!

If somebody says to you on the phone, 'I am just five minutes away from you' but is not, that is a lie. A 'white' lie is a lie! There are no white lies in Christianity. I have mentioned these examples to assert the fact that most Christians may not categorize unbelief as sin.

> ***'But without faith it is impossible to please him: for he that cometh to God must believe that he is,***

and that he is a rewarder of them that diligently seek him'...

Hebrews 11:6.

This verse clearly tells us that unbelief displeases God. If faith pleases God, then unbelief displeases Him. The life of rest is a life pillowed on the promises of God. It is a life that takes God at His word. The late Reverend Kenneth Hagin used to say 'God said it. I believe it. That settles it'. He was a man who literally took God at His word. Kenneth Hagin developed such faith that he took anything God said and believed it wholly, just exactly the way God said it.

It is not God's perfect will that anybody should die in sickness or be relieved of pain through death. Death is not the best relief and obviously not part of the rest that I am referring to here. I once listened to a message of Kenneth Hagin. In it he said that he had not been sick for forty years. Then one day as he was stepping out of his office he felt a headache. So he slapped his head and said, "No, you don't" and instantly, he was fine. That demonstrates taking God at His word!

THE LABOUR IS IN THE WORD

The concept of laboring to have rest appears paradoxical. Yet the scripture demands that from us. The 'labour' to enter this rest is a 'labour' in the word. We must meditate on the word till it takes root in us; till we totally believe it.

'For whosoever shall call upon the name of the

> ***Lord shall be saved. How then shall they call on him in whom they have not believed? And how shall they believe in him of whom they have not heard? And how shall they hear without a preacher'?...***
>
> *Romans 10:13-14.*

To labour in the word means to study and meditate on God's word daily. You should never be too busy to study the God's word.

Deuteronomy 8:3 says, '

> ***And he humbled thee, and suffered thee to hunger, and fed thee with manna, which thou knewest not, neither did thy fathers know; that he might make thee know that man doth not live by bread only, but by every word that proceedeth out of the mouth of the LORD doth man live'.***

The Bible is the source of our faith. It is the source of our Christian life. The more of the Bible we expose ourselves to, the more of God's grace and power we access.

How much of rest you enter into and enjoy largely depends on how much of God's word you believe. Those who believe doubtless enter into rest. If there is any area of your life where you do not have rest, the key to entering into rest in that area is to walk by faith in that area. To obtain faith, meditate on God's word on the subject matter.

Scriptures on healing, prosperity, etc are so popular. God's word addresses every situation in your life, even to the minute details, whether we have challenges at work or in our neighborhoods. Whatever it is, the word of God has an answer for every situation. You may not understand how the word of God has an answer to IT-related problems. You may say that the Bible does not even mention the computer. But when you sit down to meditate on God's word, He could quicken the scriptures you read and light-up what is written. That is what is called 'Rhema'. In the New Testament, two words are used in describing the word of God: *Logos* and *Rhema*.

Logos speaks of the entirety of the revelation of God. You find it used in *John 1:1* when Jesus was referred to as 'The Word of God'. '*In the beginning was the Word, and the Word was with God, and the Word was God'*. That is *Logos.*

Rhema refers to personal revelation. When you meditate on Logos, the Rhema comes to you and there is no situation nor circumstance of life that you will not find a *Rhema* for.

The Bible says ***'So then faith cometh by hearing, and hearing by the word of God'***...*Romans 10: 17.* This refers to the *Rhema.*

It takes more than *Logos* to have faith imparted to your heart. While you are meditating on *Logos, Rhema* leaps off into your heart. God speaks to you from His word. That word imparts faith to your heart. So, labour in the word of God. We are word practitioners. We do the word. A disciple is a disciplined follower. The word 'Christian' is found only once in the New Testament. The nickname was given to the followers of Jesus by Gentiles. A disciple is a strict adherent. He follows the teaching of his master strictly and whole-heartedly. He is committed and sold-out to it. The Bible is the book we should all be sold-out to.

To emphasize the utmost importance of the word, God told Joshua ***'This book of the law shall not depart out of your mouth, but you shall meditate therein day and night'***...*Joshua 1:8.*

We talk so often about meditation but do not emphasize confession. By *'this book of the law shall not depart out of your mouth,...'* what is implied is reading it out loud. This was a daily practice of those who were committed to the words of the Old Testament. They read the word of God out loud to themselves. There is something about reading it out loud to yourself. It makes those words powerful. The mouth gate is one of the most powerful gates to the human heart. Whatever is on your lips will ultimately make its way into your heart and vice versa.

Whatever is in your mouth makes way to your heart, whatever is in your heart makes way to your mouth. It is a direct connection back and forth. It is automatic. Once it is in one part, it will be found on the other end.

> ***'But what saith it? The word is nigh thee, even in thy mouth, and in thy heart: that is, the word of faith, which we preach'***
>
> *Romans 10: 8.*

I once preached a message from Mark chapter five titled

'No Boundaries'. My first point in that message was 'Do not Panic'. I illustrated with the story of Jesus going to Jairus' house to heal his daughter while the woman with the issue of blood interrupted the procession. As she was still sharing her testimony, somebody came from Jairus' house and said, *'the damsel is dead. Why trouble the Master anymore'?*

Death marks the end of life. But instantly, Jesus turned to Jairus and said, *'Be not afraid'*; do not panic. When we panic, then victory is lost and nothing can be done about a situation. Jesus said to Jairus, 'do not panic, only believe'. Jesus is saying the same thing to you now!

HOW DO YOU BELIEVE?

> ***'Faith comes by hearing and hearing by hearing the word of God'.***

If there is an area of your life where rest eludes you, search the Scriptures for promises in that particular area. When I want to search for a word, I go online and it is free of charge. When you need verses on healing or any other area, just punch on some Bible applications, and the verses would come out. Then digest those verses one after the other. Meditate on them.

The Bible in *Romans 10:8* talks about the word of faith that we preach. If faith can come to you as you meditate on the Bible and get a personal revelation, it can also come to you as you listen to messages of preachers and teachers of the Word of God. Attend services as regularly as possible. Making time only on Sundays is not good enough. Not only is the word of God being preached and taught on Sunday, it is also being preached and taught at midweek services, conferences and seminars. They are also recorded on CDs and DVDs. Buy them and listen to them over and over.

When a message relates to a very serious matter in your life, forget about every other CD, put the one that relates to you inside your car and listen to it over and over again. When you are leaving the car, take it inside your bed room or you could take a more pragmatic approach, buy three copies–one for the bedroom, one for the car, and one for the CD player in your office!

Copy that message to your laptop. Store it on your mobile phone. Wake up in the morning and pray for one hour. Then listen to that message several times over. Desperate situations call for desperate actions. People have undertaken these kind of exercises and have seen tremendous impact and results in their lives. These could only happen because faith had been imparted to them through God's Word.

Galatians 2: 20 says

> ***'I am crucified with Christ: nevertheless I live; yet not I, but Christ liveth in me: and the life which I now live in the flesh I live by the faith of the Son of God, who loved me, and gave himself for me'.***

Faith can be imparted to you through the Word of God.

Sadly, though, many people do not understand the Word of faith that we preach. They think it is every Sunday religion but it is not. That is why such people would listen to almost anybody. Do you know that it is not all the 'word of God' that is preached that is the Word of faith? If it is the word of faith, then it would be faith-building.

Listening to messages that emphasize what happened on the cross of Calvary is faith-building. I need to point out here that there are sermons you listen to that could drown or extinguish even the little faith that you have built in your heart. Many people preach traditions and unbelief. You should not listen to such messages. You should only listen to messages that would truly build your faith.

What your pastor preaches to you should be in your heart and in your mouth. That's why you have got to pay rapt attention and undivided focus on your Pastor's preaching. But how would it first settle in your heart and then be spoken out with your mouth, if you hear it only once and you do not even care to write it down? From my experience, it is what I hear over and over again and I repeatedly vocalize, that eventually makes way to my heart and is subsequently spoken out of my mouth. This is how I build my faith.

The process by which faith is imparted is an unconscious one. While you are listening to God's Word, faith builds within you. You might not be aware of this. But someday what has been built will doubtless come to the fore. Pastor David Yongi Cho told the story of a woman who had terminal cancer and had given up on life, ready to die. In the story, he told her to write 'by His stripes I am healed' 1,500 times as confession and personal application of the Word of God!

Reeling in pains, she first protested to David her unwillingness to undertake such an exercise. However, when she obeyed, she did not get to number 1,500 before the cancer disappeared! That was because while she was writing, it gradually became more and more real to her. While she was writing, she began to believe and in the middle of the assignment, she discovered the cancer had gone. This is quite instructive and buttresses the point I am making: When you believe, you enter your rest.

Let me tell the story of a Medical Doctor, Dr. Lilian Yeomans who inherited a house from her mother and decided to use that house to care for patients with terminal illnesses by feeding them with the Word of God. She asked a woman who had terminal cancer to keep repeating, without stopping, Galatians 3:13–***'Christ has redeemed us from the curse of the law, being made the curse for us, for it is written, Cursed is everyone that hangs upon the tree'.***

At the end of the first day, the terminally-ailing woman complained severely that it was not just painful, but she was feeling worse. The Doctor told her that since Doctors have already said she was going to die, she had better die speaking the word of God. So she continued to speak God's word. On the third day, the Doctor was in the kitchen preparing meals for the patients when she heard somebody stomping down the staircase, reciting the word. It was the lady, completely healed! God's word had entered into her heart and cancer had eventually died in her body. The Word became real.

Chapter 3

Obedience And Rest

'Seeing therefore it remaineth that some must enter therein, and they to whom it was first preached entered not in because of unbelief. Again, he limiteth a certain day, saying in David, Today, after so long a time; as it is said, Today if ye will hear his voice, harden not your hearts. For if Jesus had given them rest, then would he not afterward have spoken of another day. There remaineth therefore a rest to the people of God. For he that is entered into his rest, he also hath ceased from his own works, as God did from his. Let us labour therefore to enter into that rest, lest any man fall after the same example of unbelief. For the word of God is quick, and powerful, and sharper than any two edged sword, piercing even to the dividing asunder of soul and spirit, and of the joints and

> ***marrow, and is a discerner of the thoughts and intents of the heart. Neither is there any creature that is not manifest in his sight: but all things are naked and opened unto the eyes of him with whom we have to do'...***
>
> *Hebrews 4:6-13.*

When God speaks to us, we receive a personal *Rhema* and faith is birthed in our hearts. But the proof of real faith is our obedience, our stepping out to do what God has asked us to do.

In Hebrews *Chapter11* verse *8* we read:

> ***'By faith Abraham, when he was called to go out into a place which he should after receive for an inheritance, obeyed; and he went out, not knowing whither he went'.***

Psalms 23:1 says:

> ***'The LORD is my shepherd; I shall not want'.***

The satisfaction promised in the above Scripture passage is conditional. It implies that except God is the shepherd, there sure will be want. The duty of the shepherd is to provide. If truly we believe that the cross of Jesus took care of all our needs, then we can securely rest in the finished work of Calvary. That work has made abundant provision available for us. However, these provisions are location-specific. Not every place is your place.

Psalms 66:12 says:

> ***'Thou hast caused men to ride over our heads; we went through fire and through water: but thou broughtest us out into a wealthy place'.***

There sure is a wealthy place. The Bible in *I Kings 17:4* says:

> ***'And it shall be, that thou shalt drink of the brook; and I have commanded the ravens to feed thee there'.***

A wealthy place is a spiritual location in Christ Jesus. It may be a geographical location or a vocational location. Not every job is your job. Not every business is your business. Not every calling is your calling. And not every type of ministry is your ministry. God has called each of us uniquely for specific assignments. He has a unique way the calling should be carried out and a unique place where the calling should be carried out.

It is important for us to be sensitive to the Spirit of God. If a man is not sensitive to the spirit of God, he might not be able to locate what exactly is the calling of God upon his life. And he might not locate where the calling should to be carried out as well.

For Joseph, Egypt was his place. He could not have imagined in his wildest dreams that it would be Egypt. Daniel flourished in Babylon. Not every place is your place. Not every job is your job. Not every profession is your profession. Not every strategy is your strategy. Not every connection is your connection. Not every woman is your wife. Not every man is your husband. All these choices in life require spiritual direction and direction requires obedience. Basically, we need to demonstrate obedience in two ways:

1. Obedience to the written word of God

What is written is written. The written word of God is final authority. Once something is written in the Bible, it expressly reveals the will of God and there must be no argument against it. The scriptures have final authority.

2 Peter 1:21 says

> ***'For the prophecy came not in old time by the will of man: but holy men of God spake as they were moved by the Holy Ghost'.***

No scripture should be of private interpretation. Do not give your private interpretation to the word of God. Once it is written, it is written as God wanted it to be written. The Word of God is very clear and it is to be followed.

There are people who just like to argue. Peter describes them as those who *'wrest the scriptures to their destruction'(2 Peter3:16).* Some people quote the Bible out of context and say what it does not say. They do that to their own destruction. A life that is committed to what is written is a life that is positioned for rest and success.

The Bible in *Psalms 1:1-3* says:

> ***'Blessed is the man that walketh not in the counsel of the ungodly, nor standeth in the way***

> ***of sinners, nor sitteth in the seat of the scornful. But his delight is in the law of the LORD; and in his law doth he meditate day and night. And he shall be like a tree planted by the rivers of water, that bringeth forth his fruit in his season; his leaf also shall not wither; and whatsoever he doeth shall prosper'.***

The kind of man described in the above scripture has the supply of grace. The Bible says he is like a tree planted by the rivers of water, symbolic of the Holy Spirit. It means his life is anointed, the presence of God is in his life, he has the supply of the Spirit and the supply of the supernatural energy of God is his portion. The power of the Holy Ghost is also made available to him and makes him bring forth fruit in his season. All these happen because he does things according to the word and according to the supply of the Spirit. He walks in the Spirit, walks by faith and operates in the supernatural dimension of the power of God. Such a man prospers in whatever he does because he is not the one doing it. It is God who works through him. His life is described as a watered life. He is strategically planted by the river where there is rich deposit of silt. As a result, he is always nourished. There is fertility in the soil and so is he is abundantly nourished.

In Bible days there was no artificial irrigation. People planted by river banks and scattered their seeds there. The grains automatically went down to the bed of the river. Whenever the rainy season was over, the river receded and the river bank became dry ground. The river would have deposited minerals and silt, which is very fertile and rich, at the river bank.

That atmosphere became very conducive for the grains to germinate and sprout. They grew to be very healthy and brought forth abundant grains. This was because the grains were well watered. When we meditate on the Scriptures that is exactly how we are well watered. Whatever we do in obedience to the word of God, we do in the power of the Holy Ghost.

The life of rest is not a life of laziness or complete passiveness. When we labour in the word of God, it enriches us supernaturally and we have grace to act and pattern our lives according to the Word. Entering into God's rest is entering into a lifestyle of His power, presence and supernatural lifestyle. That is why *Isaiah 40 verse 31*says:

> ***'But they that wait upon the LORD shall renew their strength; they shall mount up with wings as eagles; they shall run, and not be weary; and they shall walk, and not faint'.***

The Bible tells us that *'they shall run and not be weary; they shall walk and not faint'*. This shows us that those that wait upon the Lord are not to be passive and do nothing. No, they mount up, they run, and they walk. But you know what, while they mount up and walk, they do not faint. While they run, they are not weary. This is because they are not running in their own strength or walking in their own power. They are running in the power of the Holy Ghost, and walking in the strength of God.

Who does not know that if he operates in the strength of God he will be able do much more that he can do naturally?

No wonder Paul said, ***'I labour more abundantly that they all'*** *(1corinthians 15:10).*

That grace of God will make your labour more abundant because you are not labouring in your power. Others may labour and be exhausted. They would fall out but you would still be agile, vibrant, healthy, strong and doing more. This is because your results are supernatural.

You need to live a life of obedience. Obedience does not know how to struggle. *Joshua 1: 8* says: ***'This book of the law shall not depart out of thy mouth; but thou shalt meditate therein day and night, that thou mayest observe to do according to all that is written therein: for then thou shalt make thy way prosperous, and then thou shalt have good success'.***

If what you do is as a result of the law that you meditate upon, then it is not your own idea that you are carrying out. It is not your will that you are doing; it is the will of God. It is not your idea but God's idea and you are not doing it in your power but in the power of the Holy Ghost. Your rest is in your obedience. Some people erroneously think that once you operate under the New Covenant, which is the life of grace, you really do not have to obey anything. That is not so. We are free from the Law of Moses but we are not free from the principles of God's word. The word of God is still full of principles that we have to follow.

2. Following The Angel

Exodus chapter *23:20* says

> ***'Behold, I send an Angel before thee, to keep thee in the way, and to bring thee into the place which I have prepared'.***

That is your rest, that place that is prepared by God. But the next verse says ***'Beware of him, and obey his voice, provoke him not; for he will not pardon your transgressions: for my name is in him'.***

The word 'Angel' here is 'Elohim' in the Hebrew, used for God in *Genesis 1:1*. I believe God The Father was referring to The Holy Spirit. This verse tells us to be God-conscious and to be aware that the Holy Spirit is in our lives. It tells us to recognize Him. When you do not give somebody recognition, he withdraws. We all like to go where we are celebrated and not where we are tolerated. Nobody likes to go where they would be ignored.

Isaiah 63:9-10.

> ***In all their affliction, he was afflicted, and the Angel of His presence saved them, In His love and His pity He redeemed them; And He bore them and carried them the days of old. But they rebelled and grieved His Holy Spirit; So He turned Himself against them as an enemy and He fought against them***

Anybody that is properly recognized would just be his natural self. In like manner, when the Holy Spirit is duly recognized, He speaks and operates. The Holy Spirit is sensitive. One of the symbols that represent Him is the Dove and one of the things that hurt Him is distraction. How many of us enjoy it while, right in the middle of a conversation with someone, he picks up the phone and says, 'Hello! Hello!' and then starts talking or walks away without proper taking excuse properly ? How many people like talking to people who do not give them attention? Does it not hurt? It sure does.

The Holy Spirit is a person. He has emotions and feelings and He is sensitive. He is like a dove, we are told to be aware of Him and obey His voice. If you gave instruction to someone and he did not obey, would you want to give him another instruction? All authority figures get offended when they are disobeyed.

Samuel told Saul that rebellion was equated to witchcraft, and stubbornness to idolatry in *1 Samuel 15:23* ***'For rebellion is as the sin of witchcraft, and stubbornness is as iniquity and idolatry. Because thou hast rejected the word of the LORD, he hath also rejected thee from being king'*** which is why personally, I have zero tolerance for rebellious attitudes. I just cannot endure it. When I sense rebellion, I try to get rid of it as soon as possible. It is very dangerous because satan can come in wherever there is rebellion.

Rebellion means anti-authority. The devil is anti-authority, he has no respect for rules and he has no sense of order. The enemy is the author of confusion but anywhere you see God, you will see order. The Bible says about the Holy Spirit, ***'Beware of him, obey his voice'.*** His job is to take you to the promised land. Recognizing Him and obeying His voice is the only way He would take you there.

The Lord has to be your shepherd before you can enjoy green pastures, before you can be led besides still waters and before your soul can be restored. If you do not allow Him to be your shepherd and lead you while you follow his direction, you will not make it to your rest.

Sometimes His direction does not make sense to us. Where He would tell you to go, who He will tell you to meet, may make no sense to you. Abraham was told to go to a place he did not know. When people asked him where he was going, he replied he must have replied that he did not know! He must have told those who asked him, that God would give him the map after he began the journey. People sure must have had a good laugh at him.

Romans 8:16 says

> ***'The Spirit itself beareth witness with our spirit, that we are the children of God'.***

God's plan for every life is a plan of rest, prosperity and success. However, in order to get into the place of provision, blessing and prosperity, we have to follow His direction and leading. That is why it is important for every Christian to live a life of obedience. Whatever God commands us in the word, we just must obey.

The reason why you are not able to obey some parts of the Scriptures is because you do not have faith in it. By faith Abraham obeyed. It takes faith to obey God and we should make sure that we build our faith to obey the Scriptures no matter what it says. Whether it says *'bring ye all the tithes'* or it says *'thou shall not commit adultery'* or it says *'wives submit to your own husbands'* or *'husbands love your wives'*. We must have faith and obey. Faith comes by hearing and hearing by the word of God. It is the word that you believe and are convinced of that you act upon.

Spend time in the study of God's word. Build your faith and please obey God to the letter. The blessing is in obedience. The rest you desire would be yours because you are a person who obeys God's Word.

Chapter 4

The Atmosphere Of Rest

AN ENABLING ENVIRONMENT is composed of a set of favorable, interrelated conditions–attitudes, policies, practices–that create a safe space for something to function quite easily, effectively, and efficiently.

The rest God gives and the grace He gives need an enabling environment to operate and function easily, effectively, and efficiently. Anyone who needs this rest must create these environments. Here are three particularly crucial environments you must deliberately create:

1. **The Atmosphere of Praise.**

Colossians 3:16 says

> ***'Let the word of Christ dwell in you richly in all wisdom, teaching and admonishing one another***

> ***in psalms and hymns and spiritual songs, singing with grace in your hearts to the Lord'.***

God's grace enables us to praise Him and when we do so, that grace to praise Him produces other graces. It is the grace by which we sing that produces other manifestations of God's Grace to us. One of the definitions of grace is "all of God's provision."

John 1:16 says

> ***'And of His fullness we have all received, and grace for grace'.***

Grace transports us to grace. The grace of God has many and diverse manifestations: it supplies our financial and material needs, it divinely enables us, it is what meets all the multi-faceted needs of man. However God operates by causing a manifestation of grace to lead to other manifestations of grace. One of the areas of our lives where the grace of God brings the manifestation of other graces is the grace to praise Him. Let me give you an example. I am sure you could relate with this. Sometimes you discover that a pastor is particularly exceptional and anointed while preaching than at other times. This happens because of the manifestation of grace and the anointing of the Holy Spirit.

We sing, preach and worship by the anointing of the Holy Spirit. The anointing is stronger sometimes than at other times. Songs carry grace. Benny Hinn once said 'the anointing rides on the back of songs'. This experience does not have to be limited to the congregational worship during Church services. God wants us to experience this in our own individual lives.

For you to continually experience rest, you must keep the praise of God on your lips. You must maintain a lifestyle of worship. There sure would be times when you would be tempted to be worried and weighed down. Anxiety and depression will come. But you do not have to yield to them. The Spirit of God which resides in your spirit is a singing spirit.

According to *Ephesians 5:18-19*

> ***'And do not be drunk with wine in which is dissipation but be filled with the Spirit, speaking to one another in psalms and hymns and spiritual songs, singing and making melody in your heart to the Lord'.***

It is so easy to have a flurry of songs flood you heart when you are merry or when things go well. But when you are weighed down, it is difficult to find a song. It is difficult to find the right song. In such situations, the practical way to locate the right song is to start singing the songs that you know. Eventually you will stumble on the appropriate one.

You could also start praying and singing in tongues and after some time, you could move onto praying and singing in your understanding. The song that will take you out of that heaviness will be given to you. There are songs that come to you in the night hour of life when things are difficult, bleak and challenging.

Psalms 42:8

> ***'Yet the LORD will command his lovingkindness in the daytime, and in the night his song shall be with me, and my prayer unto the God of my life'.***

In *Exodus 15:2-3*, we read

> ***'The Lord is my strength and song and He has become my salvation; He is my God and I will praise Him; my father's God and I will exalt Him. The Lord is a man of war, the Lord is His name'.***

This was Moses' song of praise after Israel had crossed the Red Sea. The Lord had first to be Moses' strength and song before He would become his salvation. The singing made God manifest. So the grace of God strengthened him in battle. The above scripture was the song the Israelites sang after they crossed the Red Sea. Moses was saying that the Lord was their strength and song before they crossed the sea and He became their salvation through the sea.

Though the Bible does not record that they people sang, yet there is reason to believe–from the progression of the song–that Moses had a song in his heart. He sang it and it brought about the manifestation of the presence and the power of God. When you sing, it brings about a divine intervention in your situation and your circumstance.

Isaiah 61:3 says

> ***'To console those who mourn in Zion, to give them beauty for ashes, the oil of joy for mourning, the garment of praise for the spirit of heaviness, that they may be called trees of righteousness, the planting of the Lord that He may be glorified'.***

Another translation says *'the mantle of praise for the spirit of heaviness'.* The mantle speaks of the anointing like the mantle of Elijah that rested on Elisha. So there is a Spirit and anointing of praise–a grace to praise God–and when that grace comes, it drives out heaviness, depression and anxiety, regardless of the situation or circumstance that you go through.

Keep a song in your heart all the time. Learn to always fill your heart with good Christian music. Do not spend all your time or a lot of your time listening to secular and worldly songs, rather listen to songs of praise and worship. What you listen to determines what you sing. Whatever you keep hearing fills your heart. Do not fill your heart with filth. Rather, fill your heart with praise. If you fill your heart with praise, you will be filled with the Spirit of praise. And if you are filled with the Spirit, you will be filled with power.

2. The Atmosphere of Prayer.

Prayer unburdens the heart of its worries. Prayer empties the heart of its cares. Paul, in his epistle to the *Philippians 4:6* tells us to ***'be anxious for nothing but in everything by prayer and supplication with thanksgiving, let your request be known***

to God'.

Some people come to church with a heavy heart because they have not yet emptied it of its worries. You may have prayed, but you need to pray long enough. You have got to pray till you cannot pray anymore. You have got to pray until something happens. You have got to pray your way to peace. We must continue till we overcome in the place of prayer.

The realm of the spirit is invisible to our physical eyes and things happen in that realm. Sometimes when you are weighed down it is indicative that things or arrangements are not in your favour in the realm of the spirit at the time. It is sometimes indicative that there are forces of darkness that are at war against you. They attack your mind and soul.

Since you cannot see what is happening in the realm of the spirit, you have got to pray. The Holy Spirit understands what is happening in that realm. When you pray in the Spirit, the Holy Ghost leads you into realms of intercession and warfare to deal with what you do not know about and definitely cannot see.

In *Romans 8:26*, we read

> ***'Likewise the Spirit also helps in our weaknesses, for we do not know what we should pray for as we ought but the Spirit Himself makes intercession for us with groaning which cannot be uttered'.***

When you pray in the Spirit, you are dealing with things in

the realm of the Spirit. When you secure victory in the Spirit, heaviness would lift and joy would burst forth. You get a note of victory in prayer when peace floods your heart. That note of victory could come in the form of laughter, joy or a song. When it comes, worry and anxiety are crushed.

Jesus was weighed down when the reality of Calvary's cross starred Him in the face. He went to the place of prayer and emptied His cares to His Father. Even though that was the very reason He was born. When the hour of death came, He did not want to go to the cross. He carried the burden of His heart to the Father at Gethsemane and as He prayed to the Father, the angel of God strengthened Him.

He got supernatural strength from the angel of God to engage in three prayer sessions. When He rose from the prayer, He was equipped and ready for what lay ahead of Him. His mood, mental condition, emotional state and the atmosphere around Him drastically changed. The resultant atmosphere of peace was ushered in through the atmosphere of prayer (Matthew 26:36-46).

3. The Atmosphere of Joy.

Keep an atmosphere of joy in your life. The Bible in *Nehemiah 8:10* says

> ***'Then he said to them, go your way, eat the fat, drink the sweet and send portions to those for whom nothing is prepared for this day is holy to our Lord. Do not sorrow for the joy of the Lord***

> ***is your strength'.***

According to *Galatians 5:22-23*

> ***'But the fruit of the Spirit is love, joy, peace, longsuffering, kindness, goodness, faithfulness, gentleness, self-control. Against such there is no law'.***

Wherever the Holy Ghost is, there is joy.

> ***'For the kingdom of God is not eating and drinking but righteousness and peace and joy in the Holy Ghost'.***
>
> *Romans 14:17.*

If you have the Holy Spirit in you, then joy should be bubbling inside you, and consequently flow from inside you, outwardly. There is joy in the Holy Ghost wherever the kingdom (rule) of God is found.

Psalm 45:6-7 declares

> ***'Your throne O God is forever and ever, a scepter of righteousness is the scepter of your kingdom. You love righteousness and hate wickedness; therefore God your God has anointed you with the oil of gladness more than your companions'.***

There is an anointing for gladness which is also an anointing of Joy. ***'To console those who mourn in Zion, to give them beauty for ashes, the oil of joy for mourning, the garment of praise for the***

spirit of heaviness that they may be called trees of righteousness, the planting of the Lord that He may be glorified'*...Isaiah 61:3.*

The word *'anointing'* in the Old Testament means to *'smear or rub against'*. It also means *'oil or fatness'*.

Isaiah 10:27 says

> ***'It shall come to pass in that day that his burden will be taken away from your shoulder and his yoke from your neck and the yoke will be destroyed because of the anointing oil'.***

The oil of joy is the anointing of joy. There is an anointing of joy that breaks the spirit of heaviness. Living in sorrow grieves the anointing of the Holy Spirit. Sorrow and the anointing do not go together. Allowing worry, depression and anxiety to weigh you down can cause miracles to move further away from you. May that not be your portion. You will enter into your rest. So keep worry, anxiety and all those tears of sorrow away from you. This is not to say there would be no problems. Every one of us faces challenges and difficult situations from time to time. But whatever they may be, do not let them weigh you down. Worries, anxiety, tears, depression, self-pity and all those negative emotions will keep you from entering your rest.

Proverbs 17:22 says'

> ***A merry heart does good like medicine but a broken spirit dries the bones'.***

It has been scientifically proven that when people laugh and are full of joy, they release certain enzymes in the body that helps the body to function well. But beyond all these, they create such a wonderful spiritual atmosphere around you that draws God's goodness and mercy, healings, miracles and divine intervention to you. So, keep an atmosphere of joy in your life.

Chapter 5

Prayer And Rest

Hebrews 4: 15–16

> ***'He was tempted as we are yet without sin, let us therefore come boldly to the throne of grace that we may obtain mercy and find grace to help in time of need'.***

In this chapter, I want to elaborate on the theme of prayer in correlative to a life of rest . The above passage of scripture is very instructive. It is an invitation–a royal invitation–as well as a command. The text lifts us aloft into the workings in the place where God lives. It describes a throne, where God sits on. It tells the type of throne. It is not the throne of judgment but the throne of grace. Justice says 'Kill him' but Mercy says 'Spare him.' Mercy sits on that throne, dispensing benefits. The throne is a place where anyone can get help. At the throne of mercy, the helpless can get help–help from whatever plagues them. It is a throne to which the needy come so their needs can be met. And it is a throne where anyone who comes there, obtains. We approach the throne through Jesus our High Priest who presents our cases on our behalf to the father.

A priest is just like everybody else. But he understands the infirmity of the people and what they are going through: their temptations, weaknesses and faults. God made Jesus the Apostle and High Priest of our profession(confession). *Hebrews 3:1* says ***'Wherefore, holy brethren, partakers of the heavenly calling, consider the Apostle and High Priest of our profession, Christ Jesus'.***

You need to know about the prayer life of Jesus because there is a connection between prayer and rest. His prayers were His petitions to God, they were His demands. But when the word '*supplication*' is used, it goes way beyond petitions to pleadings with vehement cry. This happened at the garden of Gethsemane:

'Then cometh Jesus with them unto a place called Gethsemane, and saith unto the disciples, Sit ye here, while I go and pray yonder. And he took with him Peter and the two sons of Zebedee, and began to be sorrowful and very heavy' *Matthew 26: 36-37, Mark 14:32-33, Luke 22:44.*

Have you ever felt sorrowful? Have you ever felt overwhelmed? Jesus felt that way too. You need to understand how He overcame this feeling of grief and sorrow.

In Gethsemane, Jesus stood in an intercessory role on behalf of the world. The sins of the whole world and the consequences of those sins were laid upon Him. The stark reality of what He was about to face came upon Him: the weight of sin, poverty, oppression, and sickness, apart from the physical anguish of a crown of thorns, being beaten with 39 stripes, being stripped naked and crucified.

See what He did when He was overwhelmed. The Bible tells us He went a little farther and fell on His face and prayed, *'Oh my father, if it is possible let this cup pass over me'*.

So, what do you do when life overwhelms you beyond your power and strength? What do you do when you want to run from issues yet you know it is the will of God for you to go through them? The answer is prayer! It is *PUSH*, that is, *P*raying *U*ntil *S*omething *H*appens! It is called prevailing prayer. You persist in the place of prayer till you overcome.

The Bible says in Philippians 4:6:

> ***'Be careful for nothing; but in everything by prayer and supplication with thanksgiving let your requests be made known unto God'.***

There are times when you have a difficult, nagging problem and you pray about it but your heart is as heavy when you get up from your knees as it was before you knelt down to pray. At such times prayer alone will not solve the problem. You have got to step up to *supplication*. Look at the example of Jesus;

> ***'Who in the days of his flesh, when he had offered***

> ***up prayers and supplications with strong crying and tears unto him that was able to save him from death, and was heard in that he feared'***
> *Hebrews 5:7.*

When you pour your heart out, all of your energy goes into the place of prayer. But it is not just your own energy when you start supplication prayers. You may start out in your own strength but the Holy Spirit comes to your aid, which is why I love *Romans 8:26* ***'Likewise the Spirit also helpeth our infirmities: for we know not what we should pray for as we ought: but the Spirit itself maketh intercession for us with groaning which cannot be uttered'.***

With complete translation of the word 'help' in the Greek, this passage would read ***'Likewise the spirit also takes hold together with us against our infirmities'.***

This means that the Spirit now takes hold of your weaknesses and challenges together with you. You are not the one handling this situation alone at the place of prayer. The Holy Spirit joins with you in prayer and He helps you to pray. Your flesh does not have enough energy to pray. But the Holy Ghost now begins to energize you in prayer.

The Spirit of God comes upon you, praying through you as you yield to Him. How do you yield? You yield with your will. Probably in your own strength you can only pray for 30 minutes. But He helps you to pray for one hour or more. If the matter is not taken care of in one hour, He helps you to pray for 6 hours or for 8 hours or helps you to pray every day for the next 3 months till you prevail!

In *Luke 22:39-43*, the Bible says

> ***'And he came out, and went, as he was wont, to the Mount of Olives; and his disciples also followed him. And when he was at the place, he said unto them, pray that ye enter not into temptation. And he was withdrawn from them about a stone's cast, and kneeled down, and prayed. Saying, Father, if thou be willing, remove this cup from me: nevertheless not my will, but thine, be done. And there appeared an angel unto him from heaven, strengthening him'.***

This experience Jesus had can be your experience in prayer also. Everybody needs a private place of prayer. It is good to pray together with other people as Jesus did with Peter, James and John and sometimes with the 12 disciples. But Jesus also had his private place of prayer. Even though He took Peter, James and John to pray with Him, He still moved forward beyond them.

Jesus' prayers and supplications were not done in the power of His own flesh; He prayed in the power of God, the power of the Holy Ghost–because an angel appeared to Him to strengthen Him. A lot of things happen in the realm of the spirit that we do not see with our eyes. Prayer activates the ministry of angels. When you get down to the place of prayer and you begin to pray and call upon God, angels of God will come and strengthen you in prayer. '*The angel of the Lord came from heaven, strengthening him'.*

Under that strength and anointing of prayer, He prayed more earnestly and broke through into His rest with the help of the angel of God. The Bible tells us:

> ***'Then cometh he to his disciples, and saith unto them, Sleep on now, and take your rest: behold, the hour is at hand, and the Son of man is betrayed into the hands of sinners'...***
>
> *Matthew 26:45.*

He had prayed to a point of rest in the presence of God. He had crossed what Roberts Liardon calls the 'line of confidence in the spirit realm.' Kenneth Hagin called it 'a note of victory.' It is something you just sense in your spirit that assures you that the deed is done, that the matter is settled. At that point you will not be bothered anymore even if there is no physical change in the situation.

When my wife was about to deliver our first daughter, I was worried that she had protracted labour. From false labor to delivery, it took 32 hours 20 minutes; and from real labor to delivery, it took 23 hours 20 minutes. While labour was protracted, I wasn't finding it funny! The doctors told me that she had to undergo surgery. They told me to pay and arrange for blood and injections and I did because I am not foolish.

Some born again Christians argue foolishly with doctors on such life threatening matters but when auto mechanics tell them that their car plug is bad, they do not argue! I did not argue. I agreed with them on what they wanted to do. In the heaviness of my heart, I found a quiet place and began to groan in prayer and prayed myself to a song. By the time you pray and pray and then you discover that a song has burst forth, it is *'a note of victory.'* It is a sign that you have crossed *'a line of confidence.'* It means that you have prayed yourself into God's rest. At that point, the matter is settled in the spirit realm. It would just be a matter of time before it would manifest in the natural. A few minutes after crossing that line of confidence, my wife delivered a beautiful baby girl without needing surgery. Halleluyah!

The Holy Ghost took hold together with Jesus against His infirmity and He broke through in the realm of the spirit. Jesus said, *'now let us be going; see, my betrayal is at hand'*. By the time He arrived at Gethsemane He was sorrowful but at this point, He was no longer sorrowful after prayer because He had crossed the *'line of confidence.'* He was ready to take on the cross. He literally said to the devil 'now, bring it on!'

Jesus did not only get strength to pray in the presence of God, He also got strength to go through the cross till He came out of the grave at the resurrection. Everything, including the resurrection power that would raise Him from the dead, was completely secured at Gethsemane in the place of prayer. Let us learn to pray until something happens (PUSH). Do not just talk about the situation; visit the place of prayer. Learn to spend concentrated time in the presence of God. Desperate situations call for desperate actions.

Things are happening in the realm of the spirit which we

cannot see with our eyes. Many times it is spiritual warfare that goes on there.

DANIELS FAST

In Daniel Chapter 10, Daniel had fasted and prayed for 21 days before Angel Gabriel appeared and said ***'From the very first day that you decided to chasten yourself in fasting and prayer, your prayer was answered but the Prince of Persia withstood me for 21 days'.***

There was warfare in the realm of the spirit. Eventually, Michael, one of the chief Princes, came to the aid of Angel Gabriel and he was able to overcome the demonic angel called the prince of Persia. Angel Gabriel was then able to pass through to deliver God's message to Daniel. Daniel's persistence in the place of prayer enabled angelic reinforcement. What if he had stopped praying? Gabriel would have simply gone back to heaven. Apparently, the prince of Persia was at the same level of strength with Gabriel. It must have been an arch-angel, before he could withstand Gabriel.

Every time you see Michael in the Bible, he's revealed as a warrior. In *Revelations 12:7*, Michael and his angels fought against the dragon and prevailed. Michael fought on the side of Gabriel and they overcame the prince of Persia. Interestingly, at the time Daniel had this revelation, he was in Babylon. The Kingdom of Persia was about to overcome the Kingdom of Babylon and God had revealed it to Daniel. Gabriel in his conversation with Daniel said, *"I'm going back to fight the prince of Persia."*

In other words, on his way back to heaven, he would fight again. He also said, ***"When I'm gone forth after fighting the prince of Persia and I have overcome him, the prince of Greece will come."*** This means that there are forces of darkness assigned to nations. Babylon was the world super power at that time. The Kingdom of Persia overcame Babylon and became world super power.

Historically, after the reign of Persia, Greece reigned. Those were the days of Alexandra the Great. Already in the realm of the spirit, those forces were lined up, strengthened from season to season and their role was to try to stop the plan of God. Your life is an integral part of the plan and purpose of God. You are not the only one interested in your affairs; Satan is also interested.

You can be sure that he knows what it would mean to evangelism when you prosper. If you become wealthy according to God's plan, Satan knows your kind heart, that the love of God shall abound in your heart towards the poor. They would be fed and clothed and he knows that people would be helped out of their negative circumstances. That is the last thing Satan wants, he does not want anybody helped. That is why you must stay in the place of prayer until you breakthrough in the realm of the spirit.

There are matters that could be settled in minutes. There are matters that could be settled in hours. There are matters that could be settled in days. There are matters that could be settled in weeks, month or even years. Yield to the Holy Spirit. Pray till you have 'a note of victory'. Pray until the burden leaves and you have 'an inward assurance of answered prayers' Let us learn to pray our way into rest.

Philippians 4: 6 says

> ***'Be careful for nothing; but in everything by prayer and supplication with thanksgiving let your requests be made known unto God'.***

Let the peace of God mount guard over your heart and mind. If the devil flashes a thought to cause you to worry about a matter, peace guards you. Supernatural peace protects your heart and mind. If you are still worried about an issue, you have to prevail in prayer. Get back on your knees. The Holy Spirit is ready to help you. So pray until something happens in the realm of the spirit or in the natural realm. There are times you must keep praying till you see a literal turn–around.

PUSH & KEEP PUSHING!

Pray until something happens and keep praying it does! In I Kings 18: 41–46, there had been no rain for three-and-a-half years. Elijah put his head between his knees and prayed for rain to fall. He told his servant to look towards the sea to see if there was any sign of rain, to which the servant replied on six occasions, *'I see nothing'!*

His servant kept checking on Elijah's instructions, six times and each time, he saw nothing. I believe the servant covered quite some distance in going to observe the clouds and coming to give Elijah a feedback. Elijah kept praying for hours until at the seventh time the servant said, *'I see a cloud like the hand of a man'.*

Elijah then directed his servant to tell King Ahab that there was a sound of abundance of rain. If a man's prayer caused vapor to rise from the sea and move into the clouds to form rain, your prayer can cause a car to leave Japan and make its way to Nigeria. Prayer can convene an emergency board meeting so your application could considered. Prayer can cause a man to leave the U.S. and make his way to Nigeria just to marry you. Prayer can make money to leave a bank and make its way to your life.

Prayer moves the hand that moves the world. Prayer changes things. It affects things in the realm of the spirit. It affects things in the realm of the soul and it affects things in the realm of the body.

George Muller, a great man of God, owned an orphanage. They prayed for food in the orphanage every day and one day there was no food at all. George Muller told the people in the orphanage 'go and set the table, get the children to sit around the table'. He said 'God has never failed me'. As the children sat round the table, a bang was suddenly heard from the streets. A big truck-load of food just had an accident right in front of the place. The owner came to the orphanage and said all the food should be given to the orphanage. Prayer affects the realm of the spirit, the realm of the soul and the natural realm.

Chapter 6:

Faith And Rest

JESUS TOLD A parable of the sower in *Matthew 13: 3-8*. In that parable, the seed was God's word. The seeds that fell by the wayside represented the hearts of people who heard God's word but from which the devil took the word so they would not believe and consequently, get saved. Once the word is taken, faith is taken, because the word is the word of faith.

In that same parable, Jesus said persecutions would always arise because of the word. Every time a revelation of God's word is received, there is persecution. For instance, a revelation that *'he took our infirmities and bore our sicknesses'*, would cause Satan to attack with sickness. He would want to steal that revelation from your heart. He does that by threatening you with contrary circumstances so you would not believe that the revelation is true. Faith is a product of spiritual understanding.

'And he said, unto you it is given to know the

> ***mysteries of the kingdom of God: but to others in parables; that seeing they might not see and hearing they might not understand'...***
>
> *Luke 8:10.*

This statement proves that people could look but they would not see. It is quite clear that Jesus was not talking here about physical sight. He was talking about having spiritual understanding. It therefore means that many look but not all see–spiritually. This insight is revelation knowledge. The Bible clearly teaches about the spirit of understanding and the spirit of revelation. In *Ephesians 1:17* the Bible says ***'That the God of our Lord Jesus Christ, the Father of glory, may give unto you the spirit of wisdom and revelation in the knowledge of him'.***

The Jews and Pharisees did not have the spirit of revelation in the knowledge of God but Jesus said that Spirit was given to the disciples to know the mysteries of the kingdom of God. Faith begins where the will of God is known or where the will of God is revealed. *Romans 10:17* says ***'So then, faith cometh by hearing, and hearing by the word of God'.***

In this scripture, the word *'hearing'* means inception of a message and an attainment of comprehension and understanding. When the mind of God is revealed to you, faith is birthed in your heart. Notice that faith does not come directly by the word of God; it comes by the hearing of the word of God. It is the understanding of the word you hear that engenders faith.

Do not be religious. Quite a good number of people have

a one year Bible reading plan. There is absolutely nothing wrong with that but there is something wrong when you do not read the Bible slowly and create time to understand it. Do not just open the Bible and flip through it and then not be able to remember a single verse. That would constitute an empty exercise!

When you have a revelation about healing for instance, your heart you will know that you are healed, so you will ignore the symptoms. The Reverend K.C. Price narrated how a massive growth once appeared on his chest. He said that he was too sure that by the stripes of Jesus he was healed, so he ignored the growth. Whenever he felt pain, he perceived them as lying symptoms.

The challenge is that some people did the same thing but died. This can also apply to a person who has never exercised faith and received ten thousand Naira but now believes God to provide One hundred and fifty thousand naira. Faith is not about presumption. It is not being afraid, yet pretending. No, it is coming to a point of absolute confidence, total assurance and rest because you have believed. When the devil tells you that sickness will kill you, you just laugh.

How do you build faith?

1. Pray in the Holy Ghost

Jude 20 says

> ***'But ye, beloved, building up yourselves on your***

most holy faith, praying in the Holy Ghost'.

While the word of God feeds your faith, prayer strengthens your faith. Faith is not a thing of the mind. Faith is a thing of the heart. *Romans 10:10* says ***'For with the heart man believeth unto righteousness; and with the mouth confession is made unto salvation'.***

The word *'heart'* in this passage is different from the word *'mind.'* When the Bible says that with the heart man believes, the meaning it conveys goes far deeper than the mind. What it refers to is the spirit man. For faith to be rooted in you, you have got to build your spirit. I Corinthians 14: 14 says ***'For if I pray in an unknown tongue, my spirit prayeth, but my understanding is unfruitful'.***

When you speak in tongues, it is your spirit that prays; your my mind does not understand what your spirit is saying. However, verse four of the above scripture says ***'He that speaketh in an unknown tongue edifieth himself; but he that prophesieth edifieth the church'.***

The Greek word used there is the same word used for placing one block on another, as is done when a building is erected. You develop yourself spiritually when you speak in tongues. If faith has root in your spirit, prayer then helps you to develop it. When the Bible talked about rest for Israel, it was referring to the land of Canaan–the promised land. Those who believed got into that land, while those who did not believe could not. They could not believe God and as a result, they could not enter into rest.

Spending quality time in prayer is more important than any physical activity. Prayer is very crucial to your life, especially personal prayer. It is not about attending all the prayer meetings in town. Some people hop from church to church because they heard there are 'hot' prayers going on there. What are the contents of those prayers? Are they scriptural prayers or unscriptural prayers? It is not in how much you sweat in prayers; it is faith in the word that guarantees your answers when you pray.

Some people raise prayer points that are not rooted in the scriptures. It is not only about quoting Bible verses; it is the application of the verse that matters. Several people misapply the word of God. *2 Timothy 2:15* says ***'Study to shew thyself approved unto God, a workman that needeth not to be ashamed, rightly dividing the word of truth'.***

2. Exercise Your Faith

Faith develops through exercise. There is faith in your heart, but you need to exercise it. At the time I gave my life to Christ, my family was experiencing poverty so much that we had to exercise faith for transport fare to church. For food, *'give us this day our daily bread'* was one of my favorite scriptures. After we ate dinner, my mother would not know where the next meal would come from. Then I would say to my mum 'Mummy, this is what the word of God says and I guarantee you on the strength of the word of God that by tomorrow morning, something would happen.'

We started exercising faith for a meal, taxi fares, clothes, and house rent. Sometimes it could be a disadvantage when you have everything. This is because when people are so used to having everything on a platter of gold, they will cry in the time of need because they do not know how to pray and receive provisions from God. Even when your parents are providing for you, take your faith to another level. Ask God to do things for you beyond what your parents could do, because faith needs to be exercised. Faith is believing, confessing and acting on God's word. Believe something, confess it and act on it. Exercise your faith and let it develop.

> ***'We give thanks to God always for you all, making mention of you in our prayers; Remembering without ceasing your work of faith, and labour of love, and patience of hope in our Lord Jesus Christ, In the sight of God and our father'...***
>
> *1 Thessalonians 1:2-3.*

Why was their faith growing rapidly in the midst of persecution and tribulation? The answer is simple: They accepted those persecutions as opportunities to develop their faith. There is nothing in the word of God that promises us a challenge free-life. Who do you want to resemble? Abraham? Isaac? Or Jacob? All of them faced stiff challenges.

Everything develops through use. The more you exercise your faith, the more it grows. Do you know that there are born again Christians who don't confess the word of God on a daily basis? What kind of a Christian life is that?

Hebrews 3:1 says

> ***'Wherefore, holy bre***
> ***heavenly calling, consi***
> ***Priest of our professi***

Christ remains the apostle an
today. A Christian life withou
That is not a life of faith. There is no faith without confession.

2 Corinthians 4:13 also says

> ***'We having the same spirit of faith, according as it is written, I believed, and therefore have I spoken; we also believe, and therefore speak'.***

Speak the word in every situation. Put faith-pressure on the circumstance. It will give way no matter how strong it is. No matter how high the mountain or how challenging the situation, keep confessing the word. I have done this over and over and have results to show for it. You too should continue to do exercise your faith. Do not give up. You do not have any other option to a lifestyle of faith.

What else would you do if you do not keep confessing God's word by faith? Are you going to compromise? No! Feed on the word! It sure works! The life of rest is not a life of relying on your energy and your will power. It is resting on the finished work.

HOLINESS BY FAITH

1 says

> ***'Likewise reckon ye also yourselves to be dead indeed unto sin, but alive unto God through Jesus Christ our Lord'.***

It is by meditating on the scriptures over and over that your mind gets renewed and faith is rooted in your heart. The same cross that brought forgiveness of sin, healing and prosperity in the place of sickness and poverty, is the same cross on which Jesus paid the price to break the power of sin over your life. The cross did not only forgive your sins, it broke the power of sin.

Holiness is possible by faith, not by works or by striving in the flesh nor by willpower. The more you strive, the more you will fall. Stop striving! Just focus on Jesus' finished work. If you are struggling with sinful habits, just hold firm your confession of faith and keep meditating on *Romans* Chapters *6-8*.

John 17:17 says

> ***'Sanctify them through thy truth: thy word is truth'.***

The Bible says in *Proverbs 23:7* ***'As a man thinketh in his heart, so is he'***. By consistently and daily applying God's word in your life, you will experience a totally new person evolve from your old self. It is yours for the taking.

Chapter 7

Worship And Rest

In *Leviticus 25:1-14,* we read:

> *'And the Lord spoke to Moses on Mount Sinai saying, speak to the children of Israel and say to them: When you come into the land which I give you, then the land shall keep a Sabbath to the Lord. Six years you shall sow your field and six years you shall prune your vineyard and gather its fruits but in the seventh year there shall be a Sabbath of solemn rest for the land, a Sabbath to the Lord. You shall neither sow your field nor prune your vineyard. What grows of its own accord of your harvest you shall not reap nor gather the grapes of your untended vine for it is a year for the land. And the Sabbath produce of the land shall be food for you, for you your male and female servants, your hired man*

> *and the stranger who dwells with you, for your livestock and the beasts that are in your land; all its produce shall be for food. And you shall count seven Sabbath of years for yourself seven times seven years and the time of the seven Sabbath of years shall be to you forty-nine years. Then you shall cause the trumpet of the Jubilee to sound on the tenth day of the seventh month; on the Day of Atonement you shall make the trumpet to sound throughout all your land. And you shall consecrate the fiftieth year and proclaim liberty throughout all the land to all its inhabitants. It shall be a Jubilee for you and each of you shall return to his possession and each of you shall return to his family. That fiftieth year shall be a Jubilee to you; in it you shall neither sow nor reap what grows of its own accord nor gather the grapes of your untended vine. For it is the Jubilee; it shall be holy to you; you shall eat its produce from the field. In this year of Jubilee, each of you shall return to his possession. And if you sell anything to your neighbor or buy from your neighbor's hand, you shall not oppress one another'.*

Then, in verses *20-22*, we read:

> *'And if you say, what shall we eat in the seventh year since we shall not sow nor gather in our produce? Then I will command my blessing on you in the sixth year, and it will bring forth*

> ***produce enough for three years. And you shall sow in the eighth year and eat old produce until the ninth year; until its produce comes in, you shall eat of the old harvest'.***

When God gave the Ten Commandments to Israel, He warned them to hallow the seventh day and keep it a Sabbath unto Him. The seventh day is a Sabbath. Furthermore, the last scripture above talks of the Sabbath as not just the seventh day but also the seventh year and every fiftieth year.

God wants us to understand the concept of the Sabbath. If you understand it, then you will be able to enjoy a life of rest. God instituted the Sabbath in the book of *Genesis*. He created everything in six days and rested on the seventh day. *Genesis 2:2* says ***'And on the seventh day God ended His work which He had done and He rested on the seventh day from all His work which He had done'.***

To rest means 'to cease from labour; to withdraw from work'. This is what God did on the seventh day. He sanctified the seventh day and hallowed it as a day of rest.

In the book of *Leviticus* Chapter *25*, we read about God establishing the principles and practice of Jubilee. The Old Testament was a shadow of the New Testament. The figures and representations of the Old Testament clearly pointed to the realities which would be substantiated in the New. So, not only did God institute the seventh day for rest, He also instituted the seventh and fiftieth years respectively as years of rest.

Jubilee means celebration. God declared a whole year of partying for the children of Israel. The Law of Jubilee is known as the 'Law of Perpetual Party'. The celebration starts from the first day of the year to the last day of that year. It is instructive to note that this Old Testament shadow has become a New Testament reality.

So you can walk in the fullness of this current reality. It can be your experience right now, this year, every other year and for the rest of your life. I am bold to say that this is your portion. You will celebrate. Sorrow cannot visit your home. Grief is not permitted in your heart in the name of Jesus. These are provisions of the Law of Perpetual Party.

Understand this in the light of such scriptures like Philippians 4:4 '*Rejoice in the Lord always. Again I will say, rejoice*'!

'The acceptable year of the Lord' in *Luke 4:18-19* was the year of Jubilee. ***'The Spirit of the Lord is upon Me because He has anointed Me to preach the gospel to the poor, He has sent Me to heal the brokenhearted, to proclaim liberty to the captives and recovery of sight to the blind, to set at liberty those who are oppressed, to proclaim the acceptable year of the Lord'.***

Jubilee was also called ***'the acceptable year of the Lord' or "the year of the Lord's favor."*** When God instituted it in *Leviticus 25*, it was scheduled to take place, every fiftieth year. But Jesus was anointed to proclaim Jubilee every year. By His proclamation in the above scripture, Jesus says you do not have to wait till every fiftieth year before you can enter into your rest–your Jubilee.

Jubilee is now every year. Observing Jubilee in the New Testament is different from how it was observed in the Old Testament. The reality has come and is now fulfilled in the New Testament. In the Old Testament, it was a year of restoration. Slaves were released in Jubilee. No Jew was allowed to slave for more than six years irrespective of how much he or she was bought. Because God redeemed Israel from Egypt, every slave was to be released in the seventh year. Their entitlements were to be paid to them completely. In the seventh year they are sent forth with abundance of everything the Lord has blessed their owners with while they served as slaves. In the 50th year also, every slave was to return home... *Deuteronomy 12:12-15.*

In the year of Jubilee all debts were cancelled. You were in any debts, those debts were supernaturally cancelled. The cancellation of debts was an allegory of the debt of sin we owed God. That cancellation was an apt symbolism of grace. When the grace of God kicks in, all our sins are forgiven free of charge. You do not need to fast for days for God to forgive you. Our sins are already forgiven; the blood of Jesus has paid for it. Your fast cannot pay for your sins. What Jesus did on Calvary's cross paid for them.

Debts were cancelled in the year of Jubilee. Not a single Jew was exempted from the blessing. Everyone was to be a partaker of it. In the New Testament, everybody who comes to God through the sacrifice of Jesus on Calvary's cross is entitled to the blessing of the cross. The power is in the proclamation. Once it is preached, announced or declared, it is done. There is power in the spoken word of God. *Psalms 107:20* says ***'He sent His word and healed them, and delivered them from all***

their destructions'.

God's word delivers. It totally emancipates. *John 8:31-32* says

> ***'Then Jesus said to those Jews who believed Him, if you abide in My word, you are My disciples indeed. And you shall know the truth and the truth shall make you free'.***

That's the power of God's liberating word. You, too, will totally be free. When Israel refused to obey the Law of the Sabbath and celebrate Jubilee, God sent them into exile for seventy years. In Jeremiah 25:11, we read:

> ***'And this whole land shall be a desolation and an astonishment and these nations shall serve the king of Babylon seventy years'.***

Here are three areas of rest the Sabbath brings:

1. The Sabbath speaks of Physical Rest

God told them not to work on the seventh day. During the law when its symbolism was in operation in the Old Testament, God commanded Israel to do nothing. Not even to cook! They were to eat but not to cook. They were to do absolutely no work on the Sabbath.

While it may not be the primary meaning of rest in the New Testament, it is one of the characteristics of a life at rest. A life that is truly at rest in Christ Jesus, resting on the finished work of the cross of Calvary and relying on the grace and the power of the Holy Ghost will not overdrive itself. Hard work is a common denominator in the prosperity equation. It is still a valid truism that 'the hand of the diligent shall bear rule'. God has absolutely no patience for the lazy and the slothful. *Romans 12:11* says ***'Not lagging in diligence, fervent in spirit, serving the Lord'.***

But we should not over-drive ourselves. There is a way you overdrive yourself that shows that you are depending on yourself for success. The kind of blessing we are talking about is not the one that is dependent on self but on the grace of God. Note that there is a dimension of grace that energizes you to work. But you do not have to stretch yourself beyond the grace of God upon your life…*1 Corinthians 15:10.*

In time, every wise man would discover his limits. He would know how further he should push and where and when he should slow down or completely stop. Every wise person along the journey of life should discover his rhythm and the pace at which he can move and still maintain his health optimally.

I read the book of a particular man of God who said he did not sleep more than four hours in a day. He said if you are sleeping more than four hours in a day, you are sleeping too much. He said four hours is the maximum and we should also pray for at least four hours in twenty-four hours.

When I read the book as a teenage boy, I was convicted and decided to do the same. I would set the alarm to wake me up. I was sleeping not more than four hours in a day. I did not last for two weeks. I had the most severe malaria attack in my life! Every man has his gift and capacity.

I remember my brother saying the same thing about his very hardworking mentor. He said he tried to follow his mentor's pattern since his mentor too does not sleep for more than four hours in a day. He soon found out he couldn't cope with it. I wish he asked me before he started so I could tell him my experience.

Well, some people can do it comfortably, it is by grace. If God has given you the grace to sleep just a few hours, use the grace. Make sure that you use the capacity God has given you and the potential He has equipped you with maximally. Potential should not only to be released; it should be maximized. But do not stretch yourself beyond the grace of God. Do not labor beyond your capacity.

Proverbs 10:22 says

> ***'The blessing of the Lord makes one rich and He adds no sorrow with it'.***

But when it is not the blessing of the Lord, people will become rich and sorrow will be added to it. God wants to prosper His children. The devil is the author of poverty and he is the one spreading poverty in the world. Prosperity is of God. The word 'blessed' means 'happy, prosperous and to be envied'. You will be envied in the name of Jesus. But do not forget not to overdrive yourself. It is not by power, nor by might but by the Spirit of the Lord.

As a believer you should not breakdown all the time or keep falling sick. Faith confession will not replace the law of the Sabbath, which is the law of rest. It takes your faith in God and the sacrifice of Jesus on Calvary's cross with proper nutrition and rest to live a healthy life. Do not overdrive yourself. Overdriving yourself shows you trust in yourself and not in the Almighty God.

2. The Sabbath speaks of Mental Rest

God rested on the seventh day after six days of creating the world. It was not just a physical activity; it was also a mental activity. There was nothing God proclaimed and created that He did not properly think through. Your creative faculties should also rest. You should not allow worry and anxiety to dull or kill your creative capacities. The Sabbath is a day mental rest.

Psalms 23:1-3 says

> ***'The Lord is my shepherd, I shall not want. He makes me to lie down in green pastures, He leads me beside the still waters, He restores my soul, He leads me in the paths of righteousness for His name's sake'.***

We do not only use our physical bodies when we work, we also use our souls–part of which is our minds. When we think, we exercise our mental capacities. In the process, because of the load we put on them, they expand and stretch. If we do not let our minds rest and get refreshed, we risk burnout. So we need to relax. It is good to brainstorm but that should not be the practice every day of your life.

The Bible is balanced; it talks about work and it talks about recreation. Jesus periodically scheduled times of rest with His disciples. *Mark 6:31 'And he said unto them, Come ye yourselves apart into a desert place, and rest a while:'*

Allow your soul to be renewed. The evidence of rest is a worry-free life. The Bible says in Matthew 6:34... ***'Therefore do not worry about tomorrow, for tomorrow will worry about its own things. Sufficient for the day is its own trouble'.***

God wants you to rest mentally. He does not want you to work round the clock. He wants worry out of your life completely. You need to engage your creative capacities through work but you also need to deliberately schedule times for recreation and relaxation. This is very crucial.

3. The Sabbath speaks of Spiritual Rest

Spiritual rest is found in worship. God said we should not work on the Sabbath day so we could worship. The Sabbath day is a day for worshipping God. When we worship God, we declare to Him that He is the only one on whom we depend. In worship, we exchange our strength for His strength; our power for His power and our wisdom for His wisdom. The place of worship is the place of renewal. *Psalms 95:6-7* says ***'Oh come, let us worship and bow down, let us kneel before the Lord our Maker. For He is our God, and we are the people of His pasture, and the sheep of His hand'.***

You should cultivate a life of personal worship. There is a place for corporate worship in an assembly but there is much more a place of private and personal intimacy with God. Family altars are good and very important, especially for the nurture of children. But every believer must have a private place of prayer and worship with God–a private place of devotion with Him. You should not only worship with others. If I only talk to my wife in the presence of the children and other people, then I have placed a limit on the level of our intimacy. Relationships do not grow deeper if there are no scheduled times for periodic one-on-one encounters. The closest people to you are people you have private moments with. Anybody you only speak with whenever you are in the presence of other people is not intimate with you. He can be acquainted but not intimate. One on one interaction is what brings intimacy. Nobody can be intimate with God if every time he talks to God and hears from God, it is in the gathering of His children and in the presence of other people.

God's voice comes in the place of worship. Some people wonder what the difference is between praise and worship. Praise is eulogy. I can praise a person. My wife can praise me. I can praise my wife. We can both praise God. I can thank God and I can also thank anyone I want. But I do not worship anybody except the Almighty God.

Worship is exclusively reserved for God alone. Worship is the gate which leads to intimacy–a time to de-clutter, a time to exchange and expressing affection. God wants you to express affection and adoration to Him. While it is God's express command to worship Him corporately in an assembly, you still need to schedule private times of worship with Him.

Philippians 3:3 says

> ***'For we are the circumcision who worship God in the Spirit, rejoice in Christ Jesus and have no confidence in the flesh'.***

And *John 4:23-24* says

> ***'But the hour is coming and now is it when the true worshippers will worship the Father in spirit and in truth, for the Father is seeking such to worship Him. God is Spirit and those who worship Him must worship Him in spirit and in truth'.***

How is that possible? It is possible with the help of the Holy Spirit. It is the Holy Spirit that helps our spirit to come into that realm of intimacy with God, because our spirit is the unconscious part of us. We start praising and thanking God by our own will. As we begin to do that, somewhere along the line, we enter into the dimension of worship where our spirit becomes intimate with God's Spirit.

Acts 13:2 says

> ***'As they ministered to the Lord and fasted, the Holy Spirit said, now separate to Me Barnabas and Saul for the work to which I have called them'.***

After prayer and real worship in the company of other people, if room is given, the spirit of prophecy or the gift of prophecy could manifest. The word of the Lord could come either through the minister or through somebody in the congregation. That dimension is often experienced during or after worship. When you truly worship, the Holy Spirit will speak to you. And if you follow that voice, you will find rest. There is a life of labor and there is a life of rest. Their difference is strikingly remarkable.

Chapter 8:

This Is The Rest

SOMEBODY REMARKED THAT the book of the Bible called 'Acts of the Apostles' should have been rightly named 'Acts of the Holy Spirit.' I agree with this.

In *Acts 2:1–8*, we read:

> ***'When the Day of Pentecost had fully come, they were all in one accord in one place and suddenly there came a sound from heaven as of a mighty rushing wind and it filled the whole house where they were sitting. Then there appeared to them divided tongues as of fire and one sat upon each of them. And there were all filled with the Holy Spirit and began to speak with other tongues as the Spirit gave them utterance. And there were dwelling in Jerusalem Jews, devout men from every nation under heaven. And when this***

> ***sound occurred, the multitudes came together and were confused because everyone heard them speak in his own language. Then they all amazed and marveled, saying to one another, "Look, are not all these who speak Galileans? And how is it that we hear, each in our own language in which we were born'?***

In verses *17-21* we read:

> ***'And it shall come to pass in the last days says the God, that I will pour out of My Spirit on all flesh; your sons and your daughters shall prophesy, your young men shall see visions, your old men shall dream dreams, and on My menservants and on My maidservants, I will pour out My Spirit in those days and they shall prophesy. I will show wonders in heaven above and signs in the earth beneath, blood and fire and vapour and smoke. The sun shall be turned into darkness, and the moon into blood before the coming of the great and awesome day of the Lord. And it shall come to pass that whoever calls on the name of the Lord shall be saved'***

The book of Acts is a moving story of the coming of the Holy Spirit and the indelible impact and effect that His coming brought. Many mighty miracles were done not only by the apostles but also by church officials, like deacons Phillip and Stephen. Notice that the book of Acts does not end with 'Amen.' This is quite instructive and reason is that the book is still being written. And it should not close till your own signs and wonders are recorded.

Long before this outpouring took place, the Prophet Isaiah had spoken very clearly about this would-be experience. By accurate prophetic insight, he had a sneak peek into the events that would unfold in the future and recorded it.

We read his prophetic thoughts in *Isaiah 28:11-12*.. '

> ***For with stammering lips and another tongue, He will speak to this people. To whom He said 'This is the rest with which you may cause the weary to rest and this is the refreshing.' Yet they would not hear'.***

Speaking in tongues is recorded in the very first time in scriptures in the book of *Acts chapter 2*–the scripture we first quoted in this chapter.

Notice something about speaking in tongues in *Acts chapter 2*. People who spoke in tongues did that on the day of Pentecost after they had the experience of the baptism of the Holy Spirit. It is the experience that Pentecostal Christians have, called the baptism of the Holy Ghost. That's why we–and people who have that experience–are called Pentecostals.

I mentioned earlier that speaking in tongues is a consequence of the baptism of the Holy Spirit which results in an enduement with power. *Acts 1:8* says:

> ***'But you shall receive power when the Holy Spirit has come upon you and you shall be witnesses to Me in Jerusalem and in all Judea and Samaria and to the end of the earth'.***

The word 'enduement' means 'to be clothed with power.' So, baptism in the Holy Spirit is a spiritual empowerment–an anointing experience–and the result of receiving it is that you become filled with the Holy Ghost. It is possible to be a Christian and not be baptized with the Holy Ghost.

Acts 19:1-2 states:

> ***"And it happened while Apollos was at Corinth, that Paul having passed through the upper regions came to Ephesus. And finding some disciples he said to them 'did you receive the Holy Spirit when you believed'? So they said to him 'we have not so much as heard whether there is a Holy Spirit".***

Here, Paul found certain disciples of Jesus and asked them if they had received the Holy Ghost based on his belief that they were born again. Paul actually asked them if they had received the baptism of the Holy Ghost or if they had experienced the infilling of the Holy Ghost. When someone gives his life to Christ, he automatically receives the Holy Ghost but he may not be filled with the Holy Ghost. Let me apply two illustrations that Jesus used to separate the two experiences. The first one is in *John* Chapter *4* where Jesus spoke to the woman by the well of Samaria. He asked her for a drink. The woman was shocked to hear a Jew ask her–a Samaritan–for water.

In John 4:14, Jesus said to her ***'but whoever drinks of the water that I shall give him will never thirst. But the water that I shall give him will become in him a fountain of water springing up into everlasting life'.***

He was referring to the Holy Ghost as a well of water.

John 7:38-39 says

> ***'He who believes in me as the scripture has said, out of his heart shall flow rivers of living water. But this He spoke concerning the Spirit whom those believing in Him would receive, for the Holy Spirit was not yet given because Jesus was not yet glorified'.***

One thing is common to both the well and the river and that is water. However, the difference between the well and the river is the volume or the measure of water. When you get born again, you have the Holy Spirit in a measure but the baptism in the Holy Ghost is an overflow. Speaking in tongues comes with the baptism in the Holy Ghost and that means there is a purpose for which it comes.

So, what is the purpose of speaking in tongues? There are many reasons why you should speak in tongues, but for the purpose of our study, I will focus on one and that *is Spiritual refreshing or To maintain a Spirit filled* .

THE REFRESHING

Acts 19:3-4 says

> ***'And he said to them, 'Into what then were you baptized?' So they said, 'Into John's baptism.' Then Paul said, 'John indeed baptized with a baptism of repentance, saying to the people that they should believe on Him who would come after him, that is, on Christ Jesus'.***

Paul had to explain to them the difference between the baptism of John and the baptism after the ascension of Jesus Christ. John's baptism was a baptism of cleansing; a ceremonial or symbolic cleansing. When John dipped them in water and they came out, their sins were cleansed. That exercise was to clean-up the nation and make it conducive for the Son of God to manifest.

> ***"Then Paul said 'John indeed baptized with a baptism of repentance saying to the people that they should believe on Him who would come after him, that is, Christ Jesus.' When they heard this, they were baptized in the name of the Lord Jesus and when Paul had laid hands on them, the Holy Spirit came upon them and they spoke with tongues and prophesied"...***
>
> *Acts 19:4-6.*

Ephesians 5:18 ***'And do not be drunk with wine in which is dissipation but be filled with the Spirit'.*** You need to be continually filled with the Spirit and one of the ways to do that is by speaking in tongues. Speaking in tongues was given with the baptism in the Holy Spirit so that you are not just filled once and for all. There is nothing like being filled with the Spirit once and for all, because the filling of the Spirit of God is in measures.

Water and oil are some symbols of the Holy Spirit in the Bible. Water evaporates and can also be used up. The anointing of the Holy Spirit in your life, as you put it to use, can be reduced in measure. Another symbol of the Holy Spirit is oil. Oil could lose its viscosity and its ability to lubricate. A person can be baptized with the Holy Spirit but over time spiritual power could wane in that person's life.

Acts 3:19 says

> ***'Repent therefore and be converted that your sins may be blotted out so that times of refreshing may come from the presence of the Lord'.***

We need this refreshing. When the anointing in the life of a Christian is lost and it is no longer strong, he loses the freshness that comes from the fervency of the Spirit. He loses victory in spiritual warfare. His resistance against sin becomes weak. This can happen to any believer. Every time you speak in tongues, you are renewing your experience of the baptism in the Holy Ghost. You are taking a fresh drink of spiritual water. You will experience a refreshing. You know what it means to take a cold drink on a hot day. When I am thirsty and famished and I need restoration spiritually, I switch into speaking in tongues.

Psalms 23:1-3

> ***'The Lord is my shepherd, I shall not want. He makes me to lie down in green pastures, He leads me beside the still waters, He restores my soul, He leads me in path of righteousness for His name's sake'.***

Everybody needs restoration. When a child of God is spiritually weary and he is fainting, all he needs is a fresh drink in the Holy Ghost. *Romans 12:11* ... ***'Not lagging in diligence, fervent in spirit, serving the Lord'.***

When you pray regularly in the spirit, you remain on fire for spiritual things like Bible study, church attendance, prayers, giving, volunteering and worship. Speaking in tongues helps you maintain a Spirit-filled life.

A Spirit filled life is a life lived in the REST OF GOD.

OTHER BOOKS BY HARVEST HOUSE

Abundance is a result of obeying God's laid down principles on which He founded the earth. Any deviation from these will result in scarcity on a planet of plenty. Laws govern the flow of finances and they work for whosoever complies with its provisions.

You do not need a bunch of keys to open a door; you only need the right key! This book will show you the lock's combination to financial freedom and it will steer you in the path to wealth and prosperity. Welcome to your streets of gold on this side of eternity!

When Christ sacrificed His life for us, He made provision for all we would ever need. He gave us the tool of the Communion to remind us of our covenant with Him and to enable us to activate the blessings He already purchased for us.

Jesus doesn't expect us to make light of the essence of the Communion, neither does He want us to make it a mere religious practice. Instead, He wants us to have a true revelation of what the Communion means.

In this book, learn about the Communion really means and how you can appropriately apply it for miracles in your life.

OTHER BOOKS BY HARVEST HOUSE

In the first literary work of Victor Adeyemi, he expounds God's eternal plan and purpose for each and every life.
Learn:

- Why you are the way you are
- Why you have the background you have
- How to discern times and seasons of life
- How to discover gifts, talents and anointing God has placed on your life
- How to follow God's pattern of success for your life.

Sickness is not the will of god for mankind. God's design for us is to live healthy. In this great book, you will discover:

- The origin of sickness
- How to receive healing
- How to maintain your healing
- How to heal the sick
- Biblical laws of health and much

more...

Get ready for a life with 'NO SICKNESS'

OTHER BOOKS BY HARVEST HOUSE

God wants every man to have great story in life. This is not a mere wish but something that has been worked out in details. The script of our lives always has characteristics pointers that set us on the path of manifestation. They include:

- What? Your destiny: A glorious life meant to affect the world positively.
- Why? God wants to move you from struggle and survival to relevance and significance. This is God's will for you.
- Where? Wherever God commands it, but it always stars with an encounter!
- How? God's will and way!
- When? Your defining moment, the emergency of a lifetime opportunity!
- Who? You! The world is waiting for your manifestation.

You have in these pointers vital aspects of your preordained story to ensure its manifestation. Destiny is beckoning. There is no reason in the world to let go of it. Go on, manifest!

Other Books By Harvest House

1. Prevailing Prayers
2. Rise and Be Healed
3. The Holy Spirit and You
4. Biblical Keys To Financial Overflow
5. Secrets of The Blessed
6. Evangelism That Works
7. Meanings and Mirracles of The Holy Communion
8. It's Your Time For Favour
9. Seeds of Destiny